A PAIR OF GHOSTLY HANDS

and Other Stories

Where is the most usual place to find a ghost? In a dark old house, full of shadows and mysteries? In a flower garden on a bright summer day? On a computer screen in a busy office?

In ghost stories things are never as they seem. When young Stephen's parents die, his rich cousin Mr Abney offers the boy a home. How kind of him, we think. As for vampires, everyone knows you find them in castles in Transylvania, not in pleasant English villages. And only a crazy person, surely, would choose to spend a night in a room full of murderers? Ah, but this is a museum and the murderers are only waxwork figures, so there is no possible danger. And a story about a wedding must be a happy one. What could possibly be frightening about two young people in love, getting married . . .?

But we begin with Aunt Emily, who goes to live in a pretty little house in Cornwall, not far from the sea . . .

OXFORD BOOKWORMS LIBRARY
Fantasy & Horror

A Pair of Ghostly Hands
and Other Stories
Stage 3 (1000 headwords)

Series Editor: Jennifer Bassett
Founder Editor: Tricia Hedge
Activities Editors: Jennifer Bassett and Christine Lindop

RETOLD BY DIANE MOWAT

A Pair of Ghostly Hands

and Other Stories

Illustrated by
Adam Stower

OXFORD UNIVERSITY PRESS

OXFORD

UNIVERSITY PRESS

Great Clarendon Street, Oxford OX2 6DP

Oxford University Press is a department of the University of Oxford.
It furthers the University's objective of excellence in research, scholarship,
and education by publishing worldwide in

Oxford   New York

Auckland   Cape Town   Dar es Salaam   Hong Kong   Karachi
Kuala Lumpur   Madrid   Melbourne   Mexico City   Nairobi
New Delhi   Shanghai   Taipei   Toronto

With offices in

Argentina   Austria   Brazil   Chile   Czech Republic   France   Greece
Guatemala   Hungary   Italy   Japan   Poland   Portugal   Singapore
South Korea   Switzerland   Thailand   Turkey   Ukraine   Vietnam

OXFORD and OXFORD ENGLISH are registered trade marks of
Oxford University Press in the UK and in certain other countries

ISBN 978 0 19 479125 0

Printed in China

ACKNOWLEDGEMENTS

The publisher is grateful to the following
for their kind permission to adapt copyright material:
A. P. Watt Limited (on behalf of Alice Russell, Mary Ferguson, and
W. S. O. McDowall) for *Mrs Amworth* by E. F. Benson; J. S. F. Burrage for
The Waxwork by A. M. Burrage; the Estate of Sir Arthur Quiller-Couch
for *A Pair of Ghostly Hands* (originally published as *A Pair of Hands*).

Word count (main text): 9600 words

For more information on the Oxford Bookworms Library,
visit www.oup.com/bookworms

CONTENTS

A Pair of Ghostly Hands

SIR ARTHUR QUILLER-COUCH

'Yes,' said Aunt Emily, looking dreamily into the bright fire in the fireplace. 'Oh, yes, I have seen a ghost. In fact, I lived in a house with one for several years.'

'Oh, Aunt Emily! How could you?' cried her sister's daughters.

Aunt Emily turned to look at them, and smiled. 'Ah, but my ghost wasn't at all dangerous,' she said. 'In fact,' and she looked into the fire again, 'I was sorry to lose her.'

'Oh, please tell us about her, Aunt Emily,' cried the little girls.

And this was Aunt Emily's story.

It happened when I lived in Cornwall, at Tresillack on the south coast. Tresillack was the name of a house which stood alone at the head of a valley. You could hear the sea from there, but you couldn't see it because of a little hill between the house and the sea.

The house belonged to a farmer called Mr Hosking, who lived in a farm at the foot of the valley. Several people had rented Tresillack before me, but they had all been very unpleasant people, I learnt later.

1

I told Farmer Hosking that I was a single lady and that I came from a good family. He was polite, but not at all friendly at first. Later, when I heard about the trouble that he'd had with people renting the house, I understood why.

'Well, miss,' he said finally, 'you're welcome to look at the house. The housekeeper will show you round. I'll walk up with you now, and show you where the house is.'

As I thanked him, he stopped and looked at me for a moment. Then he said, 'There's one thing I must tell you. If

'It doesn't look like a place for ghosts,' said Farmer Hosking.

you take the house, you'll have to take Mrs Carkeek too.'

'Mrs Carkeek? Is that the housekeeper?'

'Yes. She was the wife of one of my farmworkers, who died a while ago. I'm sorry, miss,' he went on, 'but I have to have a housekeeper because of . . . some things that happened. But Mary Carkeek's a nice, sensible woman, and she knows the place. Her first job was in that house, over twenty years ago. That was when Mr Kendall was the owner, before he sold the house to me.'

'Well, I'll look at the house,' I said, but I was a little unhappy about the housekeeper.

We started to walk up the valley. I don't know why, but about half-way up, I stopped and asked, 'There are no ghosts, I suppose?'

At once, I realized how stupid the question sounded, but Farmer Hosking replied seriously, 'No, I never heard of any *ghosts*.' He said the word 'ghosts' strangely, and I wondered what he meant. 'There's always been trouble with servants, of course,' he went on, 'and they talk. But Mary Carkeek lives there alone, and she seems happy enough.'

We continued to walk, and after a time, he stopped again and said, 'Look! It doesn't look like a place for ghosts.'

And it did not. It was the prettiest little house that I had ever seen. It had white walls, and there were flowering plants and climbing roses all around it. I thought it was lovely, and I began to feel much happier.

And when Mrs Carkeek opened the door, I felt happier still. She was a healthy middle-aged woman, with a kind,

3

pleasant face. We walked through the rooms together, and I found that I really liked her. The furniture was old, but the rooms were bright and clean. The house felt *loved* – I can't describe it any other way. I felt at home there immediately.

Farmer Hosking agreed to let me rent the house, and before the end of a week, I had moved into my new home.

My first month there was really happy. I was healthy and strong, and it was so enjoyable to be out of doors in the wonderful summer weather. I spent much of the time working in the beautiful garden, and usually ended my day with a walk through the cool valley to the beach and back.

I soon found that Mrs Carkeek did all the housework. She didn't talk much, and often didn't seem to listen to what I said. Her eyes had a kind of listening look, but what she was listening to, I didn't know. But she never forgot any job in the house, and she seemed to know what I wanted before I said anything. I often used to get up very early, but I always found that she had already cleaned and tidied everywhere. 'She probably gets up and starts work the minute after I go to bed,' I thought.

One day I came downstairs at four o'clock in the morning – and the house was clean and tidy. I went through to the kitchen, looking for Mrs Carkeek, but I couldn't find her anywhere. So I went upstairs and knocked on her door. There was no reply, so I knocked again. And this time a sleepy voice called out and Mrs Carkeek appeared in her night clothes, looking (I thought) very frightened.

'It's all right,' I said, 'it's not a burglar. But now I know.

'I thought you'd seen something,' cried Mrs Carkeek.

You do the housework during the night, while I'm asleep.'

Her face was white with fear. 'Oh, miss!' she cried. 'I thought you'd seen something.'

'And so I have,' I said, 'but it was neither burglars nor ghosts. Now, go back to bed and finish your sleep.'

'Thank God,' I heard her say. And she turned and went back into her room.

*   *   *

A few days later I began to understand.

On my first morning, I had found a little room at the back of the house, which had a washbasin and a tap. The day after

5

my surprise visit to Mrs Carkeek, I picked some roses from the garden. I took them into the little room and went to the washbasin to get some water. I turned on the tap – but no water came out.

I called Mrs Carkeek. 'What's wrong with this tap?' I said.

'I don't know, miss. I never use it,' she answered.

'But there must be a reason,' I said. 'Come to the back of the house with me, and we'll look at the water tanks.'

'It doesn't matter, miss. I never use it,' she said.

But I wanted to know what was wrong.

At the back of the house there was a wall, which was built against the side of a rocky hill, and further up this hill was the kitchen garden. From the garden we could look down over the wall into the water tanks. There were two – a large one for the kitchen and bathroom, and a smaller one for the little room with the washbasin. There was a pipe which went from the big tank to the small one, and although the big tank was full of water, the small one, which was lower, was empty.

'That's it!' I cried. 'There's something in the pipe and it's stopping the water from going from the big tank into the small one.' And I climbed up onto the wall.

'Don't, miss!' said Mrs Carkeek. 'I don't use that tap. I don't need it.'

'But I want it for my flowers,' I said. I felt inside the pipe. 'Ah, I thought so!' I cried, and I pulled out a cork. Immediately the water began to run into the small tank. I turned to Mrs Carkeek.

Her face was red, and her eyes were fixed on the cork in

my hand. Around it there was a piece of material with little flowers on it. It was dirty, and the colours were no longer bright. Then, as our eyes met, I remembered that two days before, Mrs Carkeek had worn a dress of the same material.

I did not show Mrs Carkeek that I had realized this, but I was very unhappy about it. Why had she lied to me?

On the second night after this, about midnight, I was lying in bed reading when I heard the sound of water running. 'It's raining,' I thought, and I got up and went to the window.

But to my surprise, it wasn't raining. The sky was clear, and the moon was high over the valley. I could hear the sea on the beach, and the air was filled with the smell of roses. But the sound of water running continued. I had to know what it was, so I took my candle and went downstairs. I followed the sound to the little room with the washbasin. Water was running from the tap.

'Mrs Carkeek has left the tap on,' I thought, so I turned it off and went back to bed. I slept for some hours, but suddenly I woke again. I realized immediately why I had woken. Water was running again. I looked at my watch and saw that it was three o'clock in the morning. Once again, I got up and went downstairs.

At the door of the little room I stopped, and then pushed the door open quickly. Mrs Carkeek wasn't there. But something *was* there, by the washbasin – something which made my heart stop beating for several seconds.

Over the washbasin and under the water running from the tap, I saw two hands.

That was all – two small hands, a child's hands. After that – nothing. They were moving quickly, washing themselves clean. They looked like real hands because I saw the water run over them – not *through* them. They were the hands of a little girl. I can't tell you how I knew, but I was sure of it.

Then the candle fell out of my hand and crashed on the floor. I stood there in the darkness, with the water running,

They were the hands of a little girl.

and I knew that I had to shut off that tap. I *had* to. With a little cry, I pushed out my hand and did it. Then I ran.

Before long it began to get light, so I washed and dressed and went downstairs. And there, at the door of the little room, I found Mrs Carkeek. She too was dressed, and she had my candle in her hand.

'Ah,' I said, 'you picked it up.'

Our eyes met. 'You knew all about it,' I continued. 'That's why you put the cork in the water pipe.'

'You saw . . .' she began.

'Yes, yes. And you must tell me all about it. Is – is it – murder?'

'Oh, no, miss! Why did you think that?'

'She was washing her hands.'

'Yes, she does that, poor child. But little Miss Margaret would never hurt anybody.'

'Miss Margaret?'

'Yes. She died when she was only seven years old. She was Mr Kendall's only daughter. That was more than twenty years ago. I was Miss Margaret's nurse, miss, so I know. She caught the illness from one of the village children.'

'But how do you know it is Margaret?'

'Those hands – how could I forget them? I was her nurse.'

'But why does she wash them?'

'Well, miss, she always liked to be clean, and all this housework, you see . . .'

I stared at Mrs Carkeek. 'Do you mean . . . Is it *Margaret* who cleans the house and does everything for me?'

Mrs Carkeek looked back at me. 'Oh, yes,' she replied.

'Poor little girl!' I said.

'Well now,' said Mrs Carkeek. 'I'm so pleased that you're not afraid. There isn't really anything to be afraid of, is there?' She looked at me hopefully. 'I'm sure she loves you, miss. But just think what a terrible time she had with the others – the people who rented the house before you.'

'Were they bad?'

'They were awful. There was a man who drank too much, and he used to run round the valley in his nightshirt. His wife drank too, and Miss Margaret had to clean after them. But they weren't the worst. There was another man and his wife, with two children. They used to beat the children and lock them in a room without food for days. You could hear their cries all up the valley. Poor little Miss Margaret saw and heard some terrible things. There was another family—'

'Stop!' I cried. 'I want to be able to sleep peacefully in this house!'

'But you won't go, miss, will you?' said Mrs Carkeek, worriedly. 'She loves you, I'm sure she does. And if you go, who knows who'll come after you? She can't leave, you see. She's been here ever since her father sold the house. He died soon after. You mustn't go!'

In fact, I had already decided to leave, but I suddenly saw how unkind that would be.

'After all,' I said, 'there's nothing to be afraid of.'

'That's right, miss,' Mrs Carkeek said. 'Nothing at all.'

*   *   *

In the end I spent three years at Tresillack, keeping the secret with Mrs Carkeek. And all that time there was love all around me. It ran through my life like a song.

Why did I ever leave the house? Because one day Farmer Hosking came to tell me that he had sold it. One of Mr Kendall's brothers was going to buy it. He was married to a good woman, and they had eight children.

'I'm sorry . . .' Farmer Hosking began.

'No,' I said. 'You're doing the right thing.'

Mrs Carkeek was going to stay, so everything was right – except that there was no place for me in the house.

'She – Margaret – will be happy now, with her cousins,' I said to Mrs Carkeek.

'Oh, yes, miss. She'll be happy,' Mrs Carkeek agreed.

So, when the time came to leave, I tried to look happy. But on the last morning, as I stood by the door, ready to go, I sent Mrs Carkeek upstairs, and I went into the little room alone.

'Margaret,' I said quietly.

There was no answer. I tried again, and this time I closed my eyes and put out both my hands.

'Margaret!' I said.

And – for a moment only – two little hands lay in mine.

Lost Hearts

M. R. JAMES

In the year 1811, at six o'clock on a fine September evening, a carriage stopped in front of Aswarby Hall. A little boy jumped out, rang the bell, and looked up at the big square house above him. Its tall, narrow windows shone with golden light in the evening sun, and all around the house was a park with great trees, which stood out against the sky. The boy looked around, and seemed pleased with what he saw.

Six months before, his parents had died, and now he had come to live at Aswarby Hall with Mr Abney, who was his cousin. Mr Abney lived alone at the Hall, and his neighbours were very surprised when he offered to give the boy a home. Mr Abney had always seemed to be interested only in his books. Indeed, he spent much of his time in his library, studying the ideas of writers who had been dead for centuries.

But when Stephen Elliott arrived at the Hall, Mr Abney seemed very welcoming, and hurried out of the library to meet his young cousin.

'How are you, my boy? How are you?' he said. 'How old are you? – I mean, you're not too tired to eat, I hope.'

'No, thank you, sir,' replied Stephen. 'I am well.'

'Good,' said Mr Abney. 'And how old are you, my boy?'

12

It seemed a little strange that he asked the same question twice in two minutes, but Stephen replied, 'I'm eleven, sir. I won't be twelve until next year, on the tenth of September.'

'The tenth of September? Nearly a year away. That's good. That's very good. I like to put these things down in my book, you see. You're sure you won't be twelve until then?'

'Yes, sir.'

'Well, well.' Mr Abney turned to his manservant, Mr

Mr Abney hurried out to meet his young cousin.

13

Parkes. 'Take him to Mrs Bunch's room, Parkes, and let him have his supper.'

Mrs Bunch was the housekeeper at Aswarby Hall. She was a round, comfortable kind of person, and in a quarter of an hour she and Stephen were good friends. She had worked at the Hall for twenty years, so she was able to answer all Stephen's questions about the house and the people in it. But some questions were easier to answer clearly than others.

One November evening Stephen was sitting by the fire in Mrs Bunch's room, when he suddenly asked, 'Is Mr Abney a good man, and will he go to heaven?'

'Good? He's the kindest person in the world! Didn't I ever tell you about the boy he took in off the street about six years ago? And the little girl the year after I came here?'

'No. Please tell me about them, Mrs Bunch,' said Stephen.

'Well,' said Mrs Bunch, 'I don't remember much about the little girl. I know that Mr Abney brought her back with him from his walk one day, and told us to take good care of her. She had no family, poor child, and she lived here with us for about three weeks. Then, one morning, she left very early, when we were all still in bed. We never saw her again.'

'And what about the little boy?' asked Stephen.

'Ah, that poor boy,' said Mrs Bunch. 'He was Italian – Giovanni, his name was. He came here one day, playing his hurdy-gurdy to get a bit of money. Mr Abney was so kind. He brought him into the house, asked him about his family, where he came from, how old he was. The boy was all alone in the world, so Mr Abney invited him to live here. But the boy did the same as the girl. One morning he disappeared. It was strange, because he didn't take his hurdy-gurdy with him, and he loved that hurdy-gurdy. It's still here.'

That night Stephen had a strange dream. His bedroom was at the top of the house, and on the same floor there was an old bathroom, which nobody used. It was always locked, but there was glass in the top of the door, so you could look in. In his dream Stephen was looking through the glass. The moon lit up the room, and Stephen could see someone in the bath, wearing something long and white. The person's body was very thin, and a strange grey colour. On the face there was a terrible little smile, and the hands lay across the heart.

As Stephen looked at it, a low cry seemed to come from its mouth, and the arms began to move. Stephen went cold with fear, and he moved back from the door. At that moment he woke up, and found that he actually was standing outside the bathroom in the moonlight. Afraid, he looked through the glass in the door to see if the terrible thing in the bath really was there. But it wasn't, and Stephen went back to bed.

The next day, Stephen told Mrs Bunch about his horrible dream. She was very interested in it, so he told Mr Abney about it too. And Mr Abney wrote it all down in his book.

*   *   *

The winter passed, and in the early spring strange things began to happen at Aswarby Hall. Mr Abney warned Stephen more than once that spring was a dangerous time for young people. 'The Greeks of two thousand years ago knew that. So take care of yourself, my boy,' he said. 'And always close your window at night.' And at about this time two things happened that Stephen always remembered.

The first was after a night when he slept very badly, although he could not remember any dreams.

The next evening he was sitting with Mrs Bunch, who was mending his nightshirt. Suddenly she held it up and said crossly, 'Stephen! How did you manage to make all these holes in your nightshirt? Look!'

All down the front of the nightshirt there were long thin holes. Stephen didn't know how they got there, but he cried, 'Oh, Mrs Bunch! They're just like the scratches on the outside of my bedroom door – but I didn't do those! I don't know where they came from!'

Mrs Bunch's mouth fell open with surprise. Then she took a candle, left the room, and hurried upstairs. When she came back, she said, 'Well, I don't know how those scratches got there. They're too high for a cat or a dog. You make sure you lock your door at night, Stephen dear!'

That was on a Friday in March, 1812.

The second thing happened the next evening. Mrs Bunch and Stephen were sitting in Mrs Bunch's room, when Mr Parkes suddenly came into the room. He didn't see Stephen at first, and his voice was much louder than usual.

'Mr Abney can get his own wine from the cellar next time! I'm not going down there again at night! I don't know what's down there – perhaps it's rats. But I tell you, I could hear them talking. I could almost hear their actual words!'

'Oh, Mr Parkes,' said Mrs Bunch. 'Rats talking, indeed!

'How did you manage to make all these holes in your nightshirt?'
said Mrs Bunch crossly.

You mustn't say things like that – you'll frighten young Stephen here to death!'

Mr Parkes suddenly realized that Stephen was there. 'Oh,' he said. 'I was just, er, having a bit of fun, Mrs Bunch. The boy knows that.'

But Stephen knew very well that it was not a bit of fun, and that Mr Parkes *had* heard something strange in the cellar.

* * *

We now come to March 24th, 1812. It was a day full of

strange things; a windy, noisy day, which filled the house and gardens with a feeling of restlessness. Out in the park in the morning, Stephen suddenly felt that there were crowds of people hurrying past him on the wind. He couldn't see them, only feel them. The wind was carrying them along, but they seemed to want to stop and hold on to the real world.

After lunch that day, Mr Abney said, 'Stephen, my boy, come and see me tonight in the library. Come at eleven o'clock. I'll be busy until that time, but I want to show you something very important. Don't tell Mrs Bunch, or any of the other servants. Just go to your bedroom at the usual time, and then come down again at eleven.'

Stephen was pleased. He liked staying up late, and he liked secrets. On his way upstairs at his usual bedtime, he looked in at the library door, wondering what it was all about. He saw a fire burning brightly, and on a table a silver cup filled with red wine. Several papers with writing on them lay nearby. Mr Abney was busy putting something on the fire, so he did not see Stephen as he passed the door.

Later in the evening the wind stopped blowing. The night became very still, and a full moon appeared. Stephen stood at his open window, looking out over the park. From time to time strange, sad little cries came from somewhere in the trees. Perhaps it was the call of night birds, Stephen thought. But no, the cries were coming nearer, and now seemed to be very close to the house. Then they stopped; but just as Stephen was going to shut the window, he saw two people in the garden below – a boy and a girl. They were standing next to each other, looking up at the windows. Stephen stared at the girl. Was she the body in the bath in his dream? His heart was cold with fear.

The girl stood still, half smiling, holding her hands over her heart. The boy, a thin shape, with black hair, slowly lifted his arms high in the air. His long fingernails shone in the hard, clear moonlight, and as he stood there with his arms up, a very frightening thing happened. On the left side of the boy's chest a great black hole slowly opened; and through the night came a long, hungry, terrible cry. The next moment, the boy and the girl disappeared.

Stephen was very frightened, but it was nearly eleven o'clock, so he decided to take his candle and go down for his meeting with Mr Abney. He hurried downstairs to the library. The door was not locked, he felt sure, because the key was on the outside as usual.

But there was no answer to his repeated knocks. He knew Mr Abney was in there, because he could hear him speaking. What was that? Why did Mr Abney try to cry out? Why was the cry suddenly cut off? Had Mr Abney, too, seen the mysterious children? But now everything was quiet, and with fear in his heart, Stephen pushed hard against the door until it opened.

*   *   *

On the table in Mr Abney's library some papers were found which explained several things to Stephen Elliott – when he was old enough to understand them. The most important sentences in the papers were these:

. . . From my reading I have learnt that centuries ago people could do strange and wonderful things. There was a man called Simon Magus, I have read, who could fly in the air, walk unseen through a crowd, call up a storm, become any animal he chose . . . He was able to do these things by first eating the heart of a boy. Another writer says that it is best to take *three* hearts, from children below the age of twelve – and to do it in the spring, when the hearts are strongest. It is important to cut out the heart from a *living* body. You then burn the heart, put the ashes in some red wine, and drink it . . .

. . . It has taken me nearly twenty years to bring my plan to a successful end. I had to find children without families who would ask difficult questions when the child disappeared. My first heart was from a girl called Phoebe Stanley – that was on March 24th, 1792. Her body is under the floor in an old bathroom at the top of the house. The second heart came from an Italian boy called Giovanni Paoli, on the night of March 23rd, 1805. His body went into the wine-cellar, behind a wall. The third and last heart must come from my cousin, Stephen Elliott. I have planned it for March 24th, 1812 . . .

. . . I have also read that there may be trouble from the ghosts, who will try to punish their killer. But how can they hurt me? I shall soon be stronger than both the living and the dead . . .

* * *

Mr Abney was found in his chair, and on his face was a look

20

Stephen pushed hard against the door until it opened.

of the most terrible anger, fear, and pain. In his left side there
was a great, open hole, through which you could see his heart.
There was no blood on his hands, and a long knife that lay
on the table was clean and bright. Perhaps some wild animal
had made that terrible wound in Mr Abney's side. The
window of the library was open, and in the end everybody
decided that a wild-cat had got in and killed Mr Abney. But
when Stephen Elliott read the papers in the library years later,
he had a very different idea about what had happened.

Mrs Amworth

E. F. BENSON

The village of Maxley, where these strange things happened last summer, lies among the gentle wooded hills of Sussex. It is a small village, but very pretty, with an old church, several shops, and lovely old houses. It is usually a quiet place, but at the weekends the peace is sadly broken by the traffic. Maxley lies on the road from London to Brighton, and our quiet village street becomes noisy and dangerous because of all the fast cars driving down to the sea for the weekend. But by Sunday night the weekend visitors have gone home, and the peace of the village returns.

I live in one of the larger village houses, and one of my neighbours is Francis Urcombe. He had been a professor at Cambridge University, but now spent all his time studying some of the stranger mysteries of life – stories of ghosts and vampires, messages from the dead, and things of that kind. 'Some people just laugh at these things,' he said to me once, 'but to many people, they are very, very real.' I also enjoy discussing things like this, so Urcombe was an interesting neighbour for me to have.

Then, last spring, another person came to live in the village. Mrs Amworth had lived in India for many years, but when her husband died, she returned to England. She came to Maxley because she wanted to live in the country, and also because a hundred years ago her family had lived there.

Mrs Amworth was a bright, likeable person, who quickly became part of our little circle of friends. She gave pleasant little lunch parties and dinner parties, and was always happy to join in a game of cards, or an evening of music and singing. Everybody liked her – except for Francis Urcombe. But he told me that he was very interested in her, and he watched and listened to her carefully all the time. I couldn't understand this because she seemed to be a very open person, with no mystery about her at all. She told us that she was forty-five, but, in fact, she looked ten years younger.

She and I often spent an evening together playing cards, either at her house or mine. Sometimes, when she came round to my house, Francis Urcombe was also with me. He never joined in our card games, but used to sit with us, smoking his pipe and watching Mrs Amworth.

One evening in July, Urcombe was in my house, and we were having a conversation about vampires. He had read a great number of books, and knew a lot about them.

'A vampire can use the body of a dead or a living person,' he told me. 'If it uses a living body, the person is no different from other people during the day. But at night the person can fly like a bat as it goes searching for the blood it needs. And when the person dies, the vampire continues to live in the dead body. Then, of course, it must stay in its grave during the day, and can only come out at night to do its terrible work. There

23

*Urcombe used to sit with us, smoking his pipe
and watching Mrs Amworth.*

are stories about vampires in every country in Europe, going back for hundreds of years. Can they *all* be untrue? I don't think so. There was a vampire here in Maxley three hundred years ago, you know. And only a year or two ago, there was a report of them in a town in northern India. So vampires are still with us, it seems.'

Just then there was a knock on my door, and I heard Mrs Amworth's friendly voice calling out. I went to let her in.

'Come in at once and save me,' I said. 'Mr Urcombe is trying to frighten me with his stories.'

'Oh, excellent!' she cried. 'I love ghost stories.'

I saw that Urcombe was watching her carefully. 'It wasn't a ghost story,' he said. 'I was talking about vampires. There's a recent report of them, for example, in India.'

For several seconds Mrs Amworth stared at Urcombe without speaking. Then she began to laugh. 'Where *did* you hear that?' she said. 'I lived in India for years and never heard anything like that. It's just a children's story.'

Urcombe began to speak, then shook his head. 'Yes, very probably,' was all he said.

In fact, he did not speak again until Mrs Amworth left. She did not seem as bright and happy as usual, and she left after only two games of cards.

When she had gone, Urcombe said, 'Her husband died in India, of course. I had forgotten that.'

After that evening, Mrs Amworth never came to see me if Urcombe was there.

*　*　*

It was a hot summer that year, with very little rain. Clouds of flying insects appeared in the evenings. They were big black things, but very quiet, so you did not feel them until they began to bite. Everybody had painful bites from these insects, usually on the neck.

In August, the son of Mrs Amworth's gardener, a boy of about sixteen, became ill. It was a mysterious illness. The boy was very pale, and was unable to work, wanting only to sleep all the time. And although he was always hungry and ate lots of good food, he became very thin. Dr Ross noticed that there were two little wounds in his neck, and thought that one of the flying insects had bitten him.

I met the doctor in the street one afternoon, and he told me that he thought that the boy was dying. 'Do you think that Mr Urcombe would see him?' he asked me. 'He may be able to help.'

Urcombe agreed, and he and Dr Ross went to see the boy that evening. Because I was alone, I went to spend the evening with Mrs Amworth. We talked of the poor boy. 'I've often been to see him,' she said, 'but I'm afraid that today was my last visit.' Her kind eyes were wet when she spoke.

Later she walked back home with me, because she wanted to borrow one of my gardening books. 'How soft and cool the night air is,' she said. 'Good clean air and gardening are the best things in life, don't you think?' She took my book and said goodnight. 'Well, work hard in the garden, sleep with your windows open at night, and you'll never be ill.'

'I always sleep with my windows open,' I said.

That night I had the most terrible dream. In my dream, I woke up and found that both my bedroom windows were closed. I jumped out of bed and went across the room to open them. But then, outside the window I saw, to my horror, Mrs Amworth's face – just her face in the darkness, close to the glass of the window, smiling at me! I turned and ran to the second window on the other side of the room. There again was Mrs Amworth's face! It was hot in the room, but what could I do? I could not open the windows and let Mrs Amworth's face come in, like some terrible, silent bird. I opened my mouth to scream – and woke up. My room was cool and quiet, with both windows open. The moon was high in the sky, and its soft light fell on my bedroom floor. But I was still afraid, and I could not sleep again.

When morning came, I slept at last, and it was late when I got up. Almost immediately, Urcombe arrived at my door.

'I want your help,' he said. 'But first I must tell you what happened last night. I went to see the boy who is ill, and he was almost dead. He was very white, with almost no blood in him. I knew at once that a vampire had taken his blood. I said that he must come to my house, and we began to carry him there. But we met Mrs Amworth in the street. When she saw that we were moving him, she was very surprised and angry.' Urcombe stopped for a minute.

'Yes, yes,' I said. 'Go on!'

'Well,' he said, 'later I put out all the lights in the room where the boy was, and I watched. One window was a little open, and, about midnight, I heard something outside,

*'When Mrs Amworth saw that we were moving the boy,
she was very surprised and angry.'*

pushing against the window. It was an upstairs room,
remember. I looked out, and there was the face of Mrs
Amworth. Her hand was on the window. Quickly, I banged
the window shut, and I think I caught her finger in it.'

'It's not possible!' I cried. 'How could she fly through the
air like that?' But then I remembered my terrible dream.

28

'I am telling you what I saw,' said Urcombe. 'All night long, until it was nearly day, she was flying outside, like some terrible bat, trying to get in.

'Now, think about these things,' he went on. 'One, I have found out the name of the town in India where the vampire report came from. Mrs Amworth and her husband lived in that same town. Two, Mrs Amworth was very angry when I moved the boy to my house. Three, she – or the vampire that lives in her body – tried to get into his room. Four, there was a vampire here in Maxley three hundred years ago. And this vampire, so the books say, was Elizabeth Chaston – and Chaston was Mrs Amworth's name before she married. Five, the boy is stronger this morning – and Mrs Amworth was not able to get to him last night.'

For a long time, we did not speak, but the horror of it became more and more real to me. Then I told Urcombe about my dream.

'It was lucky that you woke,' he said. 'You were in danger. Now, you must help me.'

'What shall I do?' I asked.

'First of all, watch this boy,' he said. 'She must not come near him. Then we must try to kill her – but it's not a person we must destroy, it's the vampire that lives in her body.'

'Is the danger only at night?' I asked.

'No,' he replied. 'Vampires that use dead bodies can't go out in daylight, but this vampire is using a living body.'

For the next twenty-four hours either Urcombe or myself was always in the room where the boy lay.

The next day was Saturday, and the weekend traffic down to Brighton was already driving fast through the village as I crossed the street on my way back to Urcombe's house. I saw him coming out of the door with a smile on his face, which told me that the boy was better. At the same time I saw Mrs Amworth coming down the street towards us.

'Good morning to you both,' she called. 'I hear the boy is doing well. I've come to sit with him for an hour. He and I are good friends.'

Urcombe looked at her, and then said, 'No! You must not sit with him, or see him. And you know why.' Then he lifted his hand and made the sign of the cross in the air.

I have never seen a face change so horribly. The skin turned grey, and at once Mrs Amworth moved back, to get away from the hand making the sign of the cross. She stepped back into the road – right in front of a fast-moving car. There was a scream, suddenly cut short, and in seconds it was all over. Mrs Amworth lay dead in the road.

* * *

Her body was taken to the cemetery outside Maxley. The village was very sad to lose Mrs Amworth in this sudden and terrible way, and only Urcombe and I, of course, knew the full story. He still seemed worried about something, but when I asked him about it, he did not answer my questions.

In November I learnt what it was. At about eleven o'clock I was walking home after a dinner with friends at the other end of the village. The moon was very bright, and I had just come to the house where Mrs Amworth once lived, when I

30

heard the sound of a door closing. The next minute, I saw her. My blood went cold. She did not see me because the trees hid me from her. She went quickly across the road, and into the garden of the house opposite. Then she was gone.

I turned and ran to Urcombe's house. The next minute, I was inside.

'What's wrong?' he asked. 'Or shall I tell you?'

'You can't guess,' I cried.

'She's come back, and you've seen her. Tell me about it.'

I told him my story.

'That's Mr Persall's house,' he said. 'Come back there with me now.'

'But what can we do?' I asked.

'I don't know. But we must go.'

The next minute, I saw her, and my blood went cold.

31

A minute later we were there. When I passed the house earlier, it was in darkness. Now there were lights in the upstairs windows. Just then, the front door opened, and Mr Persall came out. He saw us and stopped. 'I'm going to get Dr Ross,' he said. 'My wife is ill. It happened so suddenly! She went to bed before me, and, when I went up, I found her as white as a ghost, and very tired. I must go.'

'One moment,' said Urcombe. 'Was there anything on her neck?'

'How did you guess that?' said Mr Persall. 'Yes, there was a lot of blood, from two insect bites, I think they were.'

'And there's someone with her now?' asked Urcombe.

'Yes. Our servant.'

He hurried away, and Urcombe turned to me. 'I know now what we have to do,' he said. 'Go and put on some old clothes, and I'll join you at your house.'

'Where are we going?'

'To the cemetery.'

When he arrived at my house a little later, he was carrying a pick, a shovel, and a screwdriver. As we walked out of the village to the cemetery, he told me about the terrible hour that we were going to spend.

'The same vampire that lived in Mrs Amworth during her life is now using her dead body,' he said. 'That's not unusual for vampires. If I'm right, we'll find that her body hasn't changed at all.'

'But she's been dead for more than two months,' I said.

'Two months, or two years, will be the same. The vampire

"owns" her body, you see. And remember that everything we do will be to the vampire, not to Mrs Amworth's body. It's this horrible vampire that we must destroy.'

'But what are we going to do?' I asked.

'The vampire is not in her body now,' said Urcombe. 'It is out, looking for blood. But it must get back before day. When it returns, we shall wait for daylight, and then take Mrs Amworth's body out of the grave. The vampire cannot leave her body during the day. I shall use this.' He showed me the pick. 'I shall drive it straight through her heart. Then both she and the vampire will be dead. After that we must put the body back in the grave, and Mrs Amworth will be at rest at last.'

The moon was bright when we arrived at the cemetery, and we hid ourselves to wait for the vampire. The night was warm, and the hours went by quickly. By five o'clock the moon had gone, but the sky was still clear. I felt Urcombe's hand on my arm. I looked to the right and saw a woman coming towards us. She moved quickly across the cemetery, and in the starlight I could see that it was Mrs Amworth.

She stood for a minute, then stepped up on to the grave, with a low, horrible laugh, which turned my blood cold. As we watched, she held her hands high over her head and slowly disappeared, down into the grave. Urcombe took his hand from my arm.

'Come,' he said.

The ground was not hard and it did not take long to dig up the coffin. It was heavy, but in the end we pulled it up. With his screwdriver, Urcombe took off the lid, and we stood there

As we watched, Mrs Amworth slowly disappeared.

and looked down on the face of Mrs Amworth. The eyes were open, and the full, red mouth seemed to smile.

Urcombe took up his pick. 'It'll soon be finished,' he said. 'Don't look!'

I knew what was coming, but I could not look away.

Urcombe held the pick in both hands, and then brought it down hard through Mrs Amworth's heart. There was blood everywhere, and a long, terrible scream came from that full, red mouth. As the scream died away, the face changed, turning grey and thin and old.

'Thank God, that's over,' said Urcombe.

He put back the coffin lid, and as fast as we could, we lowered the coffin back into the grave and covered it over.

As we walked back to Maxley, the birds began to sing.

The Waxwork

A. M. BURRAGE

As the last visitors left Marriner's Waxworks at closing time, the manager sat in his office, talking to Raymond Hewson. The manager was well-dressed, and looked like the successful businessman that he was. Raymond Hewson's clothes were good, but were now old and tired. He was small and thin, with untidy brown hair, and he looked like a man who tried hard to be successful, but who usually failed.

'A lot of people,' said the manager, 'have asked to spend the night in the Murderers' Room. It's usually young men, and we always refuse. But you're a newspaper reporter, and that's different. People will read about the Waxworks and want to come and visit it. So that's good for business. Which newspaper do you work for?'

'Well, I don't work for just one newspaper. I'll write the story and then I'll sell it to one of them. The *Morning Echo* will probably buy it.'

'And what kind of story will you write?'

'Oh, a frightening story, of course.'

'All right then, Mr Hewson,' said the manager. 'And I'll pay you ten pounds when I see your story in the newspaper. As I said, it'll be good for business. But you won't have an easy night, you know. I know those waxwork figures very well. I've seen them dressed and undressed. In the daytime I can walk round them and feel nothing – but I couldn't spend the night alone with them.'

'Why not?' asked Hewson.

'I don't know. There isn't any reason. They were all horrible people, but these are just waxworks, not ghosts. It's just that their eyes seem to follow you . . . There's an unpleasant feeling in that room, and I think you're going to have a very uncomfortable night.'

Hewson knew that. In fact, he was afraid, but he had a wife and family, and he needed the money very badly. So he smiled at the manager and said, 'Well, I know it won't be very comfortable, because it's not a hotel room. But I don't think your waxworks will worry me very much.'

'All right, then,' said the manager. 'I think all the visitors have left now. I'll just telephone to say that the figures must not be covered tonight, and then I'll take you down and show you everything.' He spoke into the telephone for a few minutes, and turned to Hewson again. 'Please don't smoke when you're in the Murderers' Room. We thought there was a fire down there tonight. Someone rang the fire bell, but it was a mistake. And now, if you're ready, we'll go down.'

Hewson followed the manager downstairs, and through rooms where people were putting the covers on waxwork figures of kings, queens, and all kinds of famous people. The manager stopped once and asked a man in uniform to put an armchair in the Murderers' Room.

People were putting the covers on waxwork figures
of famous people.

'It's the best we can do,' he said to Hewson. 'I hope you'll be able to get some sleep.'

They went down some steps and into the Murderers' Room. It was a big room with a high ceiling, and the lights were not bright enough to reach the shadows in the corners. It was a room where you spoke in whispers, and looked behind you all the time, wondering what was there.

The waxwork murderers stood in their places with numbered tickets at their feet. They looked just like the man next door – nothing strange or different about them at all.

The manager walked round with Hewson and showed him some of the more interesting figures. Hewson stopped in front of one of them.

'Who's that?' he asked quietly.

The figure was of a small, thin man, with a little moustache and glasses. Hewson did not know why, but the figure frightened him, and he did not want to look at it again.

'Who is it?' he asked again.

'That,' said the manager, 'is Dr Bourdette.'

Hewson knew the name, but he could not remember why. 'What did he do?' he asked.

'He was French,' the manager replied. 'All Paris was afraid of him. He was a doctor by day and a murderer by night. He killed because he enjoyed killing. He always used a razor. The police knew it was him, but he was too clever for them, and they never caught him. He just disappeared. The police think he killed himself, but they never found his body.'

Hewson turned his head away. 'I don't like him at all,' he said. 'What terrible eyes he has!'

'Yes. The figure is very well done. You can feel the eyes holding you, which is very true to life, because Bourdette hypnotized the people he killed. That was the only way he could do it. He was a small man, as you see, but nobody ever tried to fight him or to escape.'

'I thought I saw him move,' said Hewson. His voice shook a little as he spoke.

The manager smiled. 'Well, we won't lock you in. You can come upstairs when you've had enough. I'm sorry the room is so dark, but you can understand why we keep it like that.'

*　*　*

The man who brought the armchair down to the Murderers' Room thought it was all very amusing.

'Where shall I put it, sir?' he asked. 'Which murderer do you want to have a little talk with tonight?'

Hewson smiled, and for a moment his fear disappeared. 'Oh, anywhere,' he said. 'I'll move it later.'

'Well, goodnight, sir,' the man said. 'I'm upstairs if you need me. Don't let them touch you with their cold hands.'

Hewson laughed and said goodnight. It was going to be easy, he thought. But he pushed the armchair round, and made sure that its back was towards Dr Bourdette. For some reason, he was more afraid of him than of the others. Suddenly he realized how silent everything was, now that the man in uniform had gone back upstairs. He understood then that it was not going to be easy after all.

In the low light the figures looked just like living people, and it seemed unnatural not to hear them breathing, or making any of the little sounds that people usually make. The air was as silent and as still as death. The only thing that moved was his own shadow.

He stared bravely at the figures in front of him. They were only waxworks. But he could feel the eyes of Dr Bourdette on his back, and it was difficult not to turn round and look.

'Come on,' he said to himself, 'if I turn and look, it will show that I'm afraid.'

He could feel the eyes of Dr Bourdette on his back.

And then another voice in his head spoke to him.

'It's because you *are* afraid that you won't turn and look at him,' it said.

The two voices argued silently for a moment, and at last Hewson turned his chair a little and looked behind him.

Among all the figures, the figure of the awful little doctor stood out strangely. Perhaps it was because the light shone straight down on him. For one horrible second, Hewson's eyes met the doctor's, and then he turned away in fear.

'He's only a waxwork like the rest of you,' Hewson said. 'You're all only waxworks.'

It was true, they were only waxworks, but waxworks don't move. Hewson hadn't actually seen them move, but he thought that in the moment when he turned to look behind him, the figures had changed place a little. But perhaps he hadn't put his chair back where it was before.

For a moment, Hewson stopped breathing, but then he said to himself, 'Calm down. Don't be stupid!' He took a notebook from his pocket and wrote quickly.

Everywhere deathly silent. Dr Bourdette's eyes. Figures seem to move when you're not watching them.

He closed the book suddenly and looked round quickly over his right shoulder. He hadn't seen or heard anything, but he felt that the figures had moved again. But of course they hadn't moved! He was being stupid. Or was he? He stood up. He'd had enough! He was going. He wasn't going to spend the night with a lot of waxworks which moved when you took your eyes off them.

42

Hewson sat down again. This was stupid. They *were* only waxworks and they *couldn't* move. He must remember that, and all would be well. Then why was there that silent, uncomfortable feeling all around him? He turned round quickly and found Dr Bourdette's eyes on him. Then, very quickly, he turned back and looked at the others. Ha! He'd nearly caught them that time.

'Just be careful! All of you!' he shouted. 'If I see one of you move, I'll break you into little pieces! Do you hear?'

He ought to go, he told himself. He already had enough for his story. But the man upstairs would laugh at him. Perhaps the manager would not give him the ten pounds, which he needed so much. Perhaps the newspaper would hear about it, and not buy his story. He thought of his wife. Was she awake? Was she thinking about him? She'd laugh when he told her about all this . . .

This was too much! The waxworks were not only moving now, they were breathing. *Somebody was breathing.* Or was it his own breathing? He sat listening. Nothing. It was his own breathing. Or had something realized that he was listening, and stopped breathing?

Hewson turned his head quickly and looked all around him, his eyes wild with fear. Everywhere he saw waxwork faces, and everywhere he felt that they had just moved, and he hadn't seen them. They were like children in class, whispering and laughing behind their teacher's back, and stopping when the teacher looked at them.

He must stop this. They were only waxworks. He tried to

think of something to bring him back to the real world of London by day. He was Raymond Hewson, an unsuccessful newspaper man, but he was a real man, and these figures were made of wax. They weren't real.

He tried to remember a funny story that he had heard yesterday, but he could feel Dr Bourdette's eyes on him. Finally, he turned his chair round to look at Dr Bourdette face to face, right into those awful, hypnotic eyes. His own eyes stared wildly, and his mouth was fixed in a terrible smile of fear. 'You moved!' he cried. 'Yes, you did! I saw you!'

Then he sat there, without moving, staring straight before him, like a man who has been turned to ice.

Dr Bourdette moved calmly and slowly. He stepped carefully down from his place and came towards Hewson. Then he smiled and said, 'Good evening.'

'It was only when I heard you talking to the manager,' he continued, speaking in excellent English, 'that I realized I was going to have someone with me here tonight. You cannot move or speak, because I have hypnotized you. You can do only what I tell you. But you can hear me. I realize that you are a little afraid, but have no fear. I am not a wax figure which has come to life, but Dr Bourdette himself.'

He stopped for a minute, then continued. 'There are reasons why I must live in England,' he said, 'and this evening I was near this building, when I saw a policeman looking at me a little too closely. I thought that he was going to follow me and start asking questions, so I hid in the crowd and came in here. I paid my money and came into this room. Then I had

'I am not a wax figure, but Dr Bourdette himself.'

a very clever idea. I shouted "Fire!" Someone rang the fire bell, and everyone ran out. When they had gone, I took the coat from my wax figure, and hid the figure under the stairs. Then I took its place.

'Since then, I have spent a very tiring evening. When people weren't looking at me, I was able to move a little and breathe deeply for a few seconds. One small boy screamed and shouted, "I saw him move!" But his parents were angry with him. "Don't tell lies!" they said.

'I had to listen to the manager talking about me, of course, but he does not really understand me. I collect things, you see. Some people collect stamps, some people collect old books. I collect necks.'

He stopped again for a moment, and looked at Hewson's neck. He did not seem to like it. 'You have a very thin neck,' he said. 'I like men with thick necks . . . thick red necks.'

He took something from his pocket, and moved it backwards and forwards across his left hand.

'This is a little French razor,' he said quietly. 'You don't see many of them in England because they don't cut very deeply – but deeply enough. You will see that for yourself in a minute. Is the razor all right for you, sir?'

He moved slowly towards Hewson. 'Please lift your chin a little,' he said. 'Thank you. A little more. Just a little more. Ah, thank you, sir, thank you . . .'

*　　*　　*

At one end of the Murderers' Room there was a window. It was made of thick glass, but a little light from the morning

46

sun came through it. This extra light only seemed to add to the horror in the room.

The waxworks stood in their places, waiting for the crowds to come in and stare at them. In the middle of the room, Hewson sat still, with his chin up and his head resting against the back of the armchair. There was no wound on his neck, nor anywhere on his body – but he was cold and dead.

Dr Bourdette stood in his place and watched the dead man. He showed no feelings, he did not move. He could not move. But then, after all, he was only a waxwork.

John Charrington's Wedding

EDITH NESBIT

No one ever thought that May Forster would marry John Charrington, but he thought differently, and when John Charrington wanted something, he usually got it. He asked her to marry him before he went to university. She laughed and refused him. He asked her again when he came home. Again she laughed and again she refused. He asked her a third time and she laughed at him more than ever.

John was not the only man who wanted to marry her. She was the most beautiful girl in our village and we were all in love with her. So none of us was pleased when John suddenly invited us to his wedding.

'Your wedding?'

'You don't mean it?'

'Who's the lucky lady? When is it?'

John Charrington waited a moment before he replied.

'Miss Forster and I will be married in September,' he said calmly.

'No, no, she's refused you again,' said someone. 'She always refuses you, John, remember?' Everyone laughed.

'No, I can see it's true,' I said, looking at his face. 'How did you do it, John?'

'The best luck in the world,' he said. 'And I never stopped asking her.'

And that was all he would say.

The strange thing was that May Forster seemed to be in love with him, too. Perhaps she had been in love with him all the time? Oh, I'll never understand women.

We were all asked to the wedding, and I was going to be best man. Everyone was talking about it and everyone asked the question, 'Does she really love him?'

At first, in the early days of summer, I asked that question myself, but after one evening in August, I never asked it again. I was going home past the church. Our church is on a hill and the grass around it is very thick and soft, so I made no sound as I walked. It was there that I saw them. May was sitting on a low gravestone with her face turned towards the evening sun, and the look on her face ended for ever any question about her love for John Charrington. She looked more beautiful than I had ever seen her.

John was lying at her feet, and it was his voice that broke the silence of the golden August evening.

'My dear, my dear, I know that I would come back from the dead if you wanted me!'

I understood now, and continued quickly on my way.

The wedding was planned for early in September. Two days before that I had to go up to London on business. As I was standing in the station, waiting for the train, I saw John Charrington and May Forster. They were walking up and down, looking into each other's eyes. Of course, I didn't speak

*The look on May's face ended for ever any question
about her love for John Charrington.*

to them, and when the train came in, I got on and found myself a seat. If John was travelling alone, I hoped he would come and talk to me.

And he did. 'Hello there,' he said, as he came into my carriage. 'That's lucky. The journey won't be boring now.'

'Where are you going?' I asked.

'To see old Branbridge, my uncle,' he answered, as he turned to say a last goodbye to May through the window.

'Oh, I wish you wouldn't go, John,' she said in a low, serious voice. 'I feel sure something will happen.'

'Do you think I'll let anything happen to me, when the day after tomorrow is our wedding day?'

'Don't go,' she asked him again.

He took her hand in his. 'I must, May. The old man's been very good to me, and now he's dying. I must go and see him, but I'll come home in good time for the wedding.'

'You're sure?' she said as the train began to move.

'Nothing will keep me away,' he replied.

When he could no longer see her, he sat down and explained that his uncle was dying at home in Peasmarsh and had asked for him. He felt that he had to go.

'I'll be back tomorrow,' he said, 'or, if not, the day after. That's plenty of time.'

'And suppose Mr Branbridge dies?'

'Alive or dead I'll be married on Thursday!' John said, opening his newspaper.

John left the train at Peasmarsh station and I watched him walk away. I went on to London where I spent the night.

When I arrived home the next afternoon, my sister said: 'Where's John Charrington?'

'Isn't he back?' I asked. I was sure he would be at home.

'No, Geoffrey. He has not returned, and, what is more, he won't. There'll be no wedding tomorrow.'

My sister always thinks badly of other people, which makes me very angry.

'Don't be stupid! Of course there'll be a wedding,' I said.

But I was not so sure when late that night John Charrington had still not returned.

The next morning the sun was shining in a clear blue sky. There was a note for me from John and when I went up to the Forsters' house, I found he had written to May too.

'Mr Branbridge asked him to stay another night,' she said. 'John's so kind, he couldn't refuse, but I wish he hadn't stayed.'

'Well, he's asked me to meet him at the station at three o'clock, and come straight on to the church,' I said.

I was at the station at half-past two. I was a little angry with John. It didn't seem right to arrive at the church straight from the train to marry that beautiful girl.

But when the three o'clock train came in and went out again without leaving any passengers, I was more than angry. There was no other train for thirty-five minutes. 'If we really hurry,' I thought, 'we should just get to the church in time. But what a stupid man to miss that first train!'

That thirty-five minutes seemed like a year as I waited. I grew more and more angry with John Charrington. The train was late, of course – and John Charrington wasn't on it.

I jumped into the carriage which was waiting outside the station. 'Drive to the church!' I said.

I was now more worried than angry. Where could he be? Was he ill? But he was never ill. Perhaps he'd had an accident. Yes, that was it. Something terrible had happened, I was sure of it. And I was going to have to tell his bride . . .

It was five to four when I reached the church. I jumped from the carriage and ran past the crowd of villagers waiting outside the church. I saw our gardener up at the front, by the door.

'Are they all still waiting, Tom?' I asked.

'Waiting, sir? No, no, the wedding's nearly finished.'

'Finished! Then Mr Charrington has come?'

'Yes, sir. He was here on time, all right. But, sir,' Tom looked around him, then spoke quietly in my ear, 'I've never seen Mr Charrington like this before. I think he's been drinking. His clothes were all dirty, and his face was as white as a sheet. People are saying all kinds of things, sir, but I think it's the drink. He looked like a ghost, and he went straight in without a word to any of us.'

The villagers were talking in whispers, and getting ready to throw their handfuls of rice over the newly married pair. Then they appeared at the church door – John Charrington and his bride. Tom was right. John Charrington was not himself. His coat was dirty, his hair untidy, and his face was deathly pale. But no paler than the face of his wife, which was as white as her wedding dress and the flowers in her hand.

As they left the church, the bell-ringers began to pull. And then came – not the happy music of wedding bells – but the long, slow, deep sound of the death bell.

Horror filled every heart in the crowd. How could the bell-ringers make so terrible a mistake? But the ringers themselves ran in fear from the church, and refused to go back in. The bride's hands were shaking, and there were grey shadows around her mouth. Her husband held her arm and walked with her through the crowd of villagers, waiting with their handfuls of rice. But the handfuls were never thrown, and the wedding bells never rang.

In a silence deeper than the silence of death, John Charrington and his bride got into their carriage, closed the door, and drove away.

At once people began to talk, full of surprise and anger and horror at what they had seen.

I drove back to the house with Mr Forster, May's father.

'Why did I let my daughter marry him?' old Forster said. 'To come to the wedding like that! I'd like to hit him in the face for doing that!'

He put his head out of the carriage window.

'Drive as fast as you can!' he shouted.

The driver obeyed. We passed the wedding carriage without looking at it, and reached home before it.

We stood at the door, in the burning afternoon sun, and a minute later the wedding carriage arrived. When it stopped in front of the steps, Mr Forster and I ran down.

'Good Heavens, the carriage is empty! But—'

*The handfuls of rice were never thrown,
and the wedding bells never rang.*

I pulled the door open at once, and this is what I saw . . .

There was no John Charrington, and all we could see of May, his wife, was something white, lying half on the floor of the carriage and half on the seat.

'I came straight here,' the driver said, as May's father lifted her out, 'and no one got out of the carriage.'

We carried her into the house in her wedding dress – and then I saw her face. How can I ever forget it? White, white, and in her eyes more fear and horror than I have ever seen on any living face. And her hair, her beautiful golden hair, was as white as snow.

As we stood there, her father and I, unable to move or speak, a boy came up to the house with a message. I took it from him and opened it.

> Mr Charrington was thrown from his horse on his
> way to the station at half past one. He was killed
> immediately.

And he was married to May Forster at the church *at half past three,* with half the village watching.

'Alive or dead, I'll be married on Thursday!'

What had happened in that carriage on the way home? No one knows – no one will ever know.

Before a week was over, they laid May Charrington beside her husband, under the soft green grass by the little church where they used to meet as lovers.

And that was the way John Charrington was married.

GLOSSARY

ashes the grey powder that is left after something has burned
bat a small animal, like a mouse with wings, that flies at night
bell-ringer someone who makes a church bell ring
best man a man at a wedding who helps the man who is getting
    married
breathe to take air in and send it out through the nose and
    mouth
bride a woman on the day of her wedding
burglar a person who goes into buildings to steal things
candle a round stick of wax that gives light when it burns
carriage a kind of 'car' that is pulled by horses
cellar a room in the ground under a house
cemetery a place where dead people are put under the ground
chest the front part of the body between the neck and stomach
chin the part of your face below your mouth
coffin the box in which a dead person is put
collect to bring together things that are the same in some way,
    to study or enjoy them
cork something you use to close a bottle or a pipe
cousin the son or daughter of your uncle or aunt; also (in this
    story) someone from your family, but not a close relation
fingernail the hard part at the end of your finger
grave *(n)* a hole in the ground where a dead person is buried
heaven the home of God (some people believe they go there
    when they die)
horrible frightening, terrible
horror a feeling of very great fear or dislike
housekeeper a person who takes care of someone's home

hurdy-gurdy a small musical instrument that is played by
    turning a handle
hypnotize (*adj* **hypnotic**) if someone hypnotizes you, you are in a
    kind of sleep, but you can still see, hear, and answer questions
insect a very small animal with six legs
material a piece of cotton, wool, etc., used for making clothes
moustache the hair above a man's mouth, below his nose
pale with little colour in the face
pick (*n*) a large tool with a sharp point, used for making holes in
    hard ground
pipe a long tube that takes water from one place to another
professor the highest level of teacher in a university
rat a small grey or brown animal with a long tail
razor a sharp thing that people use to cut hair off their bodies
rent (*v*) to pay to use another person's flat or house
rose a flower with a sweet smell
scratch (*n*) a thin cut made by something sharp
screwdriver a tool for turning screws (small pieces of sharp
    metal used for fixing things together)
servant someone who is paid to work in another person's house
shovel (*n*) a tool used for digging and moving earth with
sign of the cross a sign like this +; vampires hate this sign
    because it is a symbol of the Christian church
tank a large 'box' for water
tap something on the end of a pipe that you turn to let water out
washbasin the place in a bathroom where you wash your hands
    and face
waxwork something made from wax to look like a person
wine an alcoholic drink made from grapes
wound a hurt place in your body made by something like a gun
    or a knife

A Pair of Ghostly Hands

and Other Stories

ACTIVITIES

ACTIVITIES

Before Reading

1 **Read the back cover of the book, the story introduction on the first page, and the story titles below. How much do you know now about these stories? What kind of ghosts do you think you will find, and where will you find them? Choose from the ideas given below.**

A Pair of Ghostly Hands   *The Waxwork*
Lost Hearts   *John Charrington's Wedding*
Mrs Amworth

  1 The ghost of someone who died of a broken heart.
  2 The ghost of someone whose heart was stolen.
  3 The ghost of someone who died before their wedding.
  4 The ghost of someone who died just after their wedding.
  5 The ghost of someone who was killed during their own wedding.
  6 A ghost who has no hands.
  7 A ghost who is always washing their hands.
  8 A ghost whose hands can be seen, but nothing else.
  9 The ghost of someone who was a murderer.
 10 The ghost of someone who has become a vampire.
 11 The ghost of someone who was killed by a vampire.
 12 A ghost who appears in a castle in Transylvania.
 13 A ghost who appears in an English village.
 14 A ghost who appears in a church.

15 A ghost who appears in a prison.

16 A ghost who appears in a bathroom.

17 A ghost who appears in a museum.

18 A ghost who appears in a shopping centre.

2 **Can you guess what will happen in the stories? Choose endings for each of these sentences. (You can choose more than one if you like.)**

1 After Aunt Emily sees the ghostly hands . . .
   a) she leaves the house in Cornwall and never returns.
   b) she decides to leave, then changes her mind.
   c) she gets a priest to drive the ghost out of the house.

2 Mr Abney is kind to his cousin Stephen because . . .
   a) he has no children of his own.
   b) Stephen's parents are dead.
   c) he wants Stephen's heart.

3 After a road accident in the village of Maxley . . .
   a) a friendly ghost appears there.
   b) there are mysterious deaths in the village.
   c) a vampire has to be killed.

4 A man spends the night with some murderers because . . .
   a) he will make some money out of it.
   b) he enjoys adventure.
   c) he is too frightened to say no.

5 After John Charrington's wedding . . .
   a) John Charrington disappears.
   b) John's wife disappears.
   c) John and his wife both disappear.

While Reading

Read to the end of page 7 of *A Pair of Ghostly Hands*. Before you finish the story, make some guesses about the ghostly hands. Choose words to complete these answers.

Who do you think the ghostly hands belong to?

1 To someone that Mrs Carkeek *had / had not* known.
2 To someone in *Mr Kendall's / Farmer Hosking's* family.
3 To *a murderer / a good kind person*.
4 To *a child / an adult*.
5 To someone who died *not long / centuries* ago.

Read to the end of page 19 of *Lost Hearts*. Before you finish the story, can you guess what Stephen finds in the library? Choose T (true) or F (false) for each of these ideas.

1 Mr Abney is dead. T/F
2 Mr Abney is alive, but badly hurt. T/F
3 Mr Abney is waiting to kill him. T/F
4 The children from the garden are waiting for him. T/F
5 Mr Abney has gone, and no one ever sees him again. T/F
6 There is a knife and a wound, but no blood. T/F

Now finish reading the story. Stephen Elliott had a 'very different idea' about what had happened. What do you think this idea was? Explain it in your own words.

Read to the end of page 29 of *Mrs Amworth*. By the end of the story, who do you think will be dead? You can choose more than one answer.

1 Francis Urcombe

2 Mrs Amworth

3 The narrator

4 The son of Mrs Amworth's gardener

5 A vampire

Read to the end of page 41 of *The Waxwork*. Can you guess which of these things will be in the room at the end of the story? Choose Y (yes) or N (no) for each one.

1 A dead body Y/N

2 A razor Y/N

3 Some blood Y/N

4 The waxwork of Dr Bourdette Y/N

5 The real Dr Bourdette Y/N

Read to the end of page 51 of *John Charrington's Wedding*. These five things happen in the rest of the story. Can you guess which order they happen in?

1 John disappears.

2 John and May are married.

3 John has an accident and dies.

4 John returns to the village.

5 May dies.

After Reading

1 **Perhaps this is what some of the characters in the stories were thinking. Which characters are they (one from each story), and what has just happened in the story at this moment?**

   1 'What are they doing? Where are they taking him? Oh, that makes me so angry! I suppose they're trying to hide him from me, but he's mine, mine, mine – and I'm going to have him!'

   2 'It's nearly time. I'm so happy, so excited – and I love him so much. I didn't want him to go away, but he's back now. I can hear his footsteps, coming into the church . . .'

   3 'There – nice and clean. Now I can . . . what's that? Where did that candle come from? Oh no! She mustn't see me, she mustn't. Quickly – put the candle out.'

   4 'I hope he's going to be all right. I know I couldn't do it. I suppose he needs the money – I don't think he's got too much of that. Well, the door's not locked – he can always leave if he wants to.'

   5 'Not too long to wait now. Just a few more months and I can complete my plan. But I'm a bit worried about that dream, and of course it was *that* bathroom on the top floor where . . . But they can't do anything to stop me, surely?'

2 **Here is Mrs Carkeek talking to Farmer Hosking about Aunt Emily. Use these linking words to complete what she says.**

and / and / because / but / so / until / when / who

'Well, she knows now, Mr Hosking. Everything was fine _____ she wanted to use the tap in the little room two days ago. _____ she went to look at the water tanks, she found the cork _____ took it out. Then early this morning she got up _____ she heard water running. She went down to the little room _____ saw Margaret, _____ was washing her hands under the tap. Of course, Miss Emily was afraid at first, _____ I told her Miss Margaret loved her, _____ she decided to stay.'

3 **The day after Mr Abney died, Stephen and Mrs Bunch talked about that terrible night. Complete their conversation. (Use as many words as you like.)**

MRS BUNCH: But why did Mr Abney want to see you so late?
STEPHEN: I don't know. He just said he _____.
MRS BUNCH: It's all so strange. I don't understand it at all.
STEPHEN: And there was another strange thing, Mrs Bunch. Earlier in the evening I saw _____.
MRS BUNCH: Really? What were they like?
STEPHEN: She _____, and he _____.
MRS BUNCH: And what did they do, this boy and girl?
STEPHEN: They _____. She _____, but he _____.
MRS BUNCH: How frightening! And then you went down to the library and found poor Mr Abney in his armchair . . .

4 **This report about Mrs Amworth appeared in the local magazine after she died. Complete the text with these words (one word for each gap).**

after, dinner, enjoyed, everyone, family, friend, in, miss, quickly, returned, road, short, sorry

We are _____ to report the death of Mrs Amworth in a _____ accident. Mrs Amworth spent many years _____ India, but _____ to England earlier this year _____ the death of her husband. She came to Maxley because her _____, the Chastons, had once lived here.

In the _____ time she was with us, Mrs Amworth _____ became a part of village life and a _____ to many. Her lunch and _____ parties were popular, and she _____ card games and musical evenings. _____ in Maxley will _____ her.

5 **Did you like the ending in *The Waxwork*, or did you want to know what really happened? Choose one of the explanations below, or think of one of your own, and add a new ending.**

1 Nothing happened at all, and Hewson just frightened himself to death.

2 Hewson hypnotized himself by staring at Dr Bourdette's eyes. He then got very cold and his heart stopped beating.

3 Dr Bourdette really was there with his razor, but he didn't have to cut Hewson's neck, because Hewson died of fright.

4 The man who brought the armchair down hid in the room and later pretended to be Dr Bourdette speaking.

6 Tom the gardener in *John Charrington's Wedding* came to the Forsters' house to ask Geoffrey (the narrator) what had happened. Put their conversation in the right order, and write in the speakers' names. Tom speaks first (number 3).

1 _____ 'Half past one! But at half past three he was in the church, getting married! We all saw him!'

2 _____ 'No, Tom, she isn't all right, and I don't think she ever will be again.'

3 _____ 'What's happened, sir? People are saying that Mr Charrington has disappeared.'

4 _____ 'I know, Tom. So did I. That's what's so terrible.'

5 _____ 'What did the message say, sir?'

6 _____ 'I'm afraid he has, Tom. You see, when we got back here to the house, there was a message about him.'

7 _____ 'So that poor, poor girl married a ghost, and rode home with him in the carriage. Is she . . .?'

8 _____ 'It said . . . It said that Mr Charrington was killed in an accident on his way to the station. At half past one.'

7 Here are some more titles for the five stories. Decide which title goes with which story, and think of one more title for each story. Which title do you like best, and why?

- Twice Dead
- Keeping a Promise
- A Tap in the Night
- The Eyes of a Murderer
- Ashes for Mr Abney
- A Lucky Bride
- A Job in the Cemetery
- A Dangerous Spring
- A Gentle Ghost
- The Neck Collector

ABOUT THE AUTHORS

E. F. BENSON
Edward Frederic Benson was born in 1867. He was one of three brothers who all became writers; unusually, all three of them wrote ghost stories as well as novels and other works. Benson is best known for his 'Lucia' books, which are amusing stories about life in an English village, but he was also very successful at writing ghost stories, and he wrote a great number of them. He died in 1940.

A. M. BURRAGE
Alfred McLellan Burrage was born in Middlesex in England in 1889 and died in 1956. He was a journalist, poet, and short-story writer, who wrote more than fifty ghost stories. *The Waxwork* was published in the collection *Someone in the Room* in 1931. Using the pen-name 'Ex-Private X' he also wrote *War is War*, a novel based on his experiences in the First World War in France.

M. R. JAMES
Montague Rhodes James was born in Kent in 1862. He was a very clever student, and spent his life teaching and writing in two great colleges – King's College, Cambridge, and Eton College, a famous boys' school. He is best remembered today for his ghost stories (five of them are retold in a Stage 4 Bookworm, *The Unquiet Grave*). He only wrote about thirty of them, but many

people think he is one of the best writers of ghost stories that there has ever been. Many other writers, then and since, studied his stories carefully and tried to make theirs as good. He died in 1936.

EDITH NESBIT

Edith Nesbit was born in London in 1858. In 1880 she married Hubert Bland, and when he became ill Edith had to work to make money for them both. She began writing poems and stories for newspapers, and went on writing all her life. She is best known for her stories for children (*Five Children and It* and *The Railway Children* are both retold in Bookworms), but she also wrote very good ghost stories. *John Charrington's Wedding* was written in 1891, and was published in the collection *Grim Tales* in 1893. Edith Nesbit died in 1924.

SIR ARTHUR QUILLER-COUCH

Arthur Quiller-Couch was born in Cornwall in 1863 and was educated at Oxford University. His first novel, *Dead Man's Rock*, was published in 1887, and he went on to write many novels, poems, and books and papers about the teaching of English. In 1900 he edited the first *Oxford Book of English Verse*, and in 1912 he became a Professor of English at Cambridge University. He loved Cornwall, and often used it as the background for his stories and novels. He died in 1944.

OXFORD BOOKWORMS LIBRARY

Classics • Crime & Mystery • Factfiles • Fantasy & Horror
Human Interest • Playscripts • Thriller & Adventure
True Stories • World Stories

The OXFORD BOOKWORMS LIBRARY provides enjoyable reading in English, with a wide range of classic and modern fiction, non-fiction, and plays. It includes original and adapted texts in seven carefully graded language stages, which take learners from beginner to advanced level. An overview is given on the next pages.

All Stage 1 titles are available as audio recordings, as well as over eighty other titles from Starter to Stage 6. All Starters and many titles at Stages 1 to 4 are specially recommended for younger learners. Every Bookworm is illustrated, and Starters and Factfiles have full-colour illustrations.

The OXFORD BOOKWORMS LIBRARY also offers extensive support. Each book contains an introduction to the story, notes about the author, a glossary, and activities. Additional resources include tests and worksheets, and answers for these and for the activities in the books. There is advice on running a class library, using audio recordings, and the many ways of using Oxford Bookworms in reading programmes. Resource materials are available on the website <www.oup.com/bookworms>.

The *Oxford Bookworms Collection* is a series for advanced learners. It consists of volumes of short stories by well-known authors, both classic and modern. Texts are not abridged or adapted in any way, but carefully selected to be accessible to the advanced student.

You can find details and a full list of titles in the *Oxford Bookworms Library Catalogue* and *Oxford English Language Teaching Catalogues*, and on the website <www.oup.com/bookworms>.

STARTER • 250 HEADWORDS

present simple – present continuous – imperative –
can/cannot, must – going to (future) – simple gerunds …

Her phone is ringing – but where is it?

Sally gets out of bed and looks in her bag. No phone. She looks under the bed. No phone. Then she looks behind the door. There is her phone. Sally picks up her phone and answers it. *Sally's Phone*

STAGE 1 • 400 HEADWORDS

… past simple – coordination with *and*, *but*, *or* –
subordination with *before, after, when, because, so* …

I knew him in Persia. He was a famous builder and I worked with him there. For a time I was his friend, but not for long. When he came to Paris, I came after him – I wanted to watch him. He was a very clever, very dangerous man. *The Phantom of the Opera*

STAGE 2 • 700 HEADWORDS

… present perfect – *will* (future) – *(don't) have to, must not, could* –
comparison of adjectives – simple *if* clauses – past continuous –
tag questions – *ask/tell* + infinitive …

While I was writing these words in my diary, I decided what to do. I must try to escape. I shall try to get down the wall outside. The window is high above the ground, but I have to try. I shall take some of the gold with me – if I escape, perhaps it will be helpful later. *Dracula*

... should, may – present perfect continuous – *used to* – past perfect –
causative – relative clauses – indirect statements ...

Of course, it was most important that no one should see
Colin, Mary, or Dickon entering the secret garden. So Colin
gave orders to the gardeners that they must all keep away
from that part of the garden in future. ***The Secret Garden***

STAGE 4 • 1400 HEADWORDS

... past perfect continuous – passive (simple forms) –
would conditional clauses – indirect questions –
relatives with *where/when* – gerunds after prepositions/phrases ...

I was glad. Now Hyde could not show his face to the world
again. If he did, every honest man in London would be proud
to report him to the police. ***Dr Jekyll and Mr Hyde***

STAGE 5 • 1800 HEADWORDS

... future continuous – future perfect –
passive (modals, continuous forms) –
would have conditional clauses – modals + perfect infinitive ...

If he had spoken Estella's name, I would have hit him. I was so
angry with him, and so depressed about my future, that I could
not eat the breakfast. Instead I went straight to the old house.
Great Expectations

STAGE 6 • 2500 HEADWORDS

... passive (infinitives, gerunds) – advanced modal meanings –
clauses of concession, condition

When I stepped up to the piano, I was confident. It was as if I
knew that the prodigy side of me really did exist. And when I
started to play, I was so caught up in how lovely I looked that
I didn't worry how I would sound. ***The Joy Luck Club***